BERLIN
Masterpieces of Architecture

BERLIN

Masterpieces of Architecture

Andras Kaldor

ANTIQUE COLLECTORS' CLUB

First published 2002
© 2002 Andras Kaldor
World copyright reserved

ISBN 1 85149 362 X

British Library Cataloguing-in Publication Data
A catalogue record for this book is available from the British Library

Frontispiece: Deutscher Dom, see pp.62–63
Title page: Mohrenkolonnaden, Mohrenstrasse

Printed in Italy
Published in England by the Antique Collectors' Club Limited
Woodbridge, Suffolk IP12 4SD

Contents

Foreword   7

Acknowledgements   9

Introduction   10-11

Map   12-13

1.   Schloss Charlottenburg   14-15

2.   Sammlung Berggruen   16-17

3.   Käthe-Kollwitz-Museum   18-19

4.   Ludwig-Erhard-Haus   20-21

5.   Theater des Westens   22-23

6.   Kaiser-Wilhelm-Gedächtniskirche   24-25

7.   Zoologischer Garten   26-27

8.   Bauhaus-Archiv   28-29

9.   Siegessäule   30-31

10. Schloss Bellevue   32-33

11. Haus der Kulturen der Welt   34-35

12. Deutscher Bundestag - Reichstag   36-39

13. Shell-Haus   40

14. Neue Nationalgalerie   41

15. St.-Matthäus-Kirche   42-43

16. Philharmonie und Kammermusiksaal   44-45

17. Brandenburger Tor   46-47

18. Humboldt-Universität   48-49

19. Neue Wache   50-51

20. Staatsoper   52-53

21. Alte Bibliothek   54-55

22. St.-Hedwigs-Kathedrale   56-57

23. Französischer Dom   58-59

24. Konzerthaus   60-61

25. Deutscher Dom   62-63

26. Altes Museum   64-65

27. Alte Nationalgalerie   66-67

28. Berliner Dom   68-69

29. Sony-Center   70-71

30. Jüdisches Museum   72-73

31. Aldo-Rossi-Block   74-75

32. Märkisches Museum   76-77

33. Nikolaikirche   78-79

34. Berliner Rathaus   80-81

35. Fernsehturm   82-83

36. Hackesche Höfe   84-85

37. Neue Synagoge   86-87

38. Friedrichstadtpalast   88-89

39. Deutsches Theater   90-91

40. Hamburger Bahnhof   92-93

Bibliography   94

Jägerstraße Nos. 59 & 60

FOREWORD

Rolls-Royce is delighted to sponsor Andras Kaldor's book on the architecture of Berlin. These notable paintings illustrate the vibrancy and diversity of this great city.

To service the world's aerospace industry, the Dahlewitz facilities of Rolls-Royce Deutschland were established in 1993 with an investment of DM420m. In total, Rolls-Royce has invested more than DM2bn in Germany.

Rolls-Royce employs about 2,300 people in Germany in Berlin/Brandenburg, Hesse, Hamburg and Schleswig-Holstein, and supports many more jobs among its suppliers. The company is helping to keep high-tech engineering in Germany at the leading edge of global development.

Rolls-Royce is delighted to be playing a part in modern Germany and proud to be part of its future.

John Rose
Chief Executive
Rolls-Royce plc

Hausvogteinplatz Nos. 3 & 4

To Sally, companion on all my travels,
and to my grandchildren Jack, Ava, Finlay, Oliver, Imogen and Oscar man

ACKNOWLEDGEMENTS

Special thanks to John Rose at Rolls-Royce for his generous support, my Berlin friends Susanne Bader and Kai Uwe Peter for their companionship and help, and Elizabeth Knoll of the publisher Nicolai for helping me with some source material for the book.

Nikolaikircheplatz

Philip-Johnson-Haus, Friedrichstrasse 200

INTRODUCTION

The city that has experienced practically everything within living memory of its inhabitants is bound to be of interest to the visitor. As a Hungarian, I have lived through similar experiences; in Berlin it all got exaggerated: the various 'isms' were harsher, the defeats heavier, the depression longer, and when the Berlin Wall collapsed, the joy and relief greater, although not quite as all would have wanted it.

Berlin today is a great and vibrant city, and in this book I've drawn and painted some of the buildings that have made an impression on me during my many visits. The first time I went there was to research my book *Great Opera Houses* – the Staatsoper on the Unter den Linden is one of Europe's great institutions and the first building I painted in Berlin.

When drawing and painting a building, it is necessary to understand the thought process of the architect designing it. In Berlin, specially with the buildings of the nineteenth

U-Bahnhof Wittenbergplatz

century, the source of inspiration is evident, yet there is an unmistakable Germanic quality in the adaptations. A design influenced by, say, the Renaissance, looks different in New York, or Paris – or Berlin; the difference is influenced by climate, available materials, and most of all, in Berlin, by the German spirit of solid strength and durability.

Those interested in contemporary architecture will be entirely satisfied by a visit, for large parts of the city are being rebuilt, and much of it resembles a massive construction site, but not for long, judging by the speed with which things are going up. The world's architects are gathered in Berlin to show off their talents, mostly to critical acclaim, though in some instances not to everyone's liking. The new Berlin will take some time to settle down – for the newly-planted linden trees to reach maturity, the Schlossplatz to be sorted out, and the trams to run again to the Ku'damm. Then the reunification of the city will be complete.

Straße des 17. Juni

Alt-Moabit

Kurfürstendamm

The numbers in red circles correspond to those used in
the headings within this book.

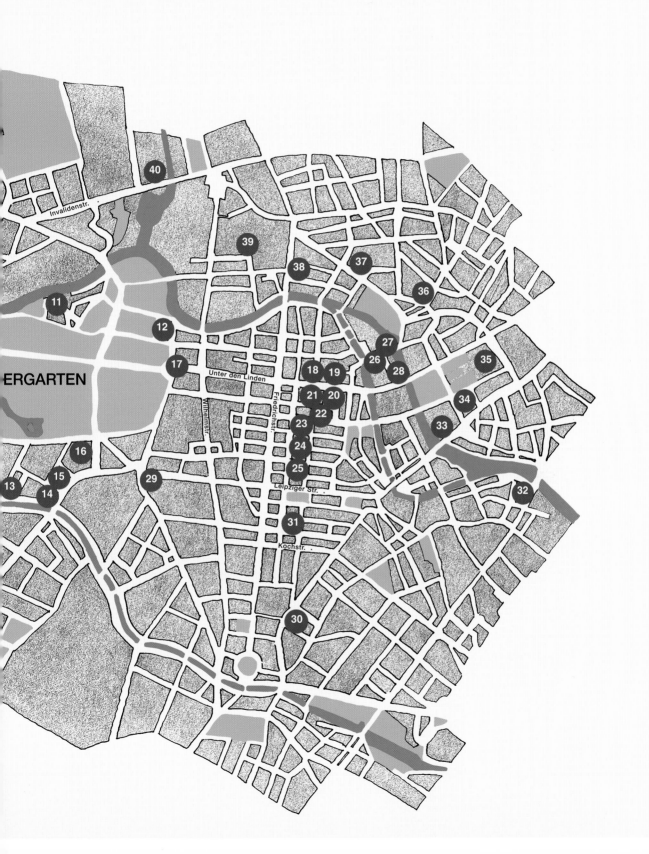

1. Schloss Charlottenburg

Designed by Johann Arnold Nering in 1695 as a modest summer residence for Sophie Charlotte, the future wife of the Elector Friedrich III. The palace was extended 1701–13 by Johann Eosander von Göthe who also added the cupola and the orangery. Friedrich II (the Great) added the east wing, designed by Georg Wenzeslaus von Knobelsdorff 1740–46.

The equestrian bronze in the courtyard of the Great Elector, Friedrich Wilhelm, is by Andreas Schlüter, 1697.

Belvedere

2. SAMMLUNG BERGGRUEN
Schlossstraße Charlottenburg

In 1855, Friedrich August Stüler was commissioned by Friedrich Wilhelm IV to design the two buildings to house the royal stables and to form an architectural link to the palace.

The museum, holding the collection of Heinz Berggruen, opened in 1966 and is known for its many paintings, drawings and gouaches by Picasso, sculptures by Laurens and Giacometti, and many famous paintings. The collection was given to Berlin by Heinz Berggruen on his return to his native city from Paris.

Fasanenstraße No. 26

3. KÄTHE-KOLLWITZ-MUSEUM

Fasanenstraße 25

This elegant tree-lined street has attracted some of Berlin's most exclusive shops, as well as having some fine *fin de siècle* villas. No. 24 is the Käthe-Kollowitz Museum exhibiting the artist's drawings, posters and sculptures. No. 25 is an auction house and art gallery built in 1892.

In the 1960s the street was threatened with demolition to make way for road improvements, but the emerging movement to preserve some of the best buildings of this part of the city prevailed and the buildings have been saved.

Fasanenstraße Nos. 24 & 25

4. LUDWIG-ERHARD-HAUS

Fasanenstraße

British architect Nicholas Grimshaw designed this high-tech building for the Berlin Stock Exchange and Chamber of Commerce. Completed in 1998, the main structure is of fifteen elliptical arches following the irregular shape of the site. The floors are suspended by steel cables from the arches, allowing complete freedom to design the layout of the offices and circulation spaces. The temperature-sensitive glass louvres control the temperature inside the building.

5. THEATER DES WESTENS
Kantstraße

Described as exhibiting many of the elements of the history of architecture, the Theater des Westens was designed by the architect Bernhard Sehring, and built in 1896. The façade contains Neo-Classical and Palladian elements, with the odd Art Nouveau detail here and there. The back and the sides have Romanesque battlements, half-timbered walls and pointed roofs.

The restoration of the building was recently completed, with the exception of the Emperor's Staircase from the garden to the ornate lobby and the Delphi Kino building.

6. KAISER-WILHELM-GEDÄCHTNISKIRCHE

Breitscheidplatz

The original Neo-Romanesque church was designed by Franz Schwechten, and consecrated in 1895 in memory of Kaiser Wilhelm I. The west tower that remained standing after allied bombing in 1943 has become a famous landmark, surrounded by the new commercial area of the Europa Center at the end of the Kurfürstendamm. The new octagonal church by Egon Eiermann was built in 1963.

The history of the church is documented in the memorial hall at the base of the tower.

7. ZOOLOGISCHER GARTEN
Budapester Straße

The zoo was founded in 1841 by Martin Lichtenstein and Peter Joseph Lenné in the south-west corner of the Tiergarten. Of the many architect-designed animal habitats only a few remained after the war. The oriental Elephant Gate on Budapester Strasse, one of the main entrances, is next to one of the largest aquariums in Europe.

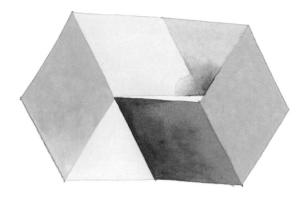

8. BAUHAUS-ARCHIV
Klingelhöferstraße

The Bauhaus school was founded in Weimar by Walter Gropius in 1919, and moved to Dessau in 1925 where it provided inspiration and set standards in educating artists and architects.

This Walter Gropius designed building of 1964 was intended for a site in Darmstadt, but when the archive moved to Berlin, modifications were needed to fit the new location. After the death of Gropius in 1969, the work was carried out between 1971 and 1978 by his long-time associate Alec Cvijanovic. The building houses the archive, library and occasional exhibitions.

9. SIEGESSÄULE
Großer Stern

Erected in 1873 to commemorate the victory in the war against the Danes in 1864, the Austrians in 1866, and the French in 1871, this 69 metre high triumphal column now stands at the Grosser Stern in Tiergarten. Originally it stood in front of the Reichstag, but was moved to its present position in 1938. The gilded sculpture of Victory on the top of the column is by Friedrich Drake. The bronze relief panels at the base removed after the war, were returned by France in 1987 for the 750th anniversary of the founding of Berlin.

10. SCHLOSS BELLEVUE
Spreeweg

Built in 1786 for Prince August Ferdinand, youngest brother of Friedrich the Great, the castle was used as a royal residence until 1861. It was subsequently converted, first to house the Museum

of German Ethnology and then in 1938 to accommodate guests of the government. It suffered severe war damage and was reconstructed between 1955 and 1959.

Since the reunification of Germany in 1990, Schloss Bellevue has been the official residence of the President of the German Federal Republic.

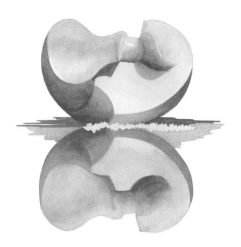

11. HAUS DER KULTUREN DER WELT

John-Foster-Dulles-Allee

The American entry in the international architecture competition of 1957, the building was designed by Hugh Stubbins as a conference hall. The roof, supported at only two points, collapsed in 1980, and after the structural problems were solved, the building was reconstructed. It reopened in 1989 as a centre for world culture.

The Henry Moore sculpture, *Butterfly*, was a 750th anniversary present to Berlin from the German Government.

12. DEUTSCHER BUNDESTAG – REICHSTAG

Platz der Republik

Since October 1991, the Reichstag is once again the seat of the German Parliament, and once again the symbol of German unity, thus fulfilling its original purpose. The Neo-Renaissance building was designed by Paul Wallot and was built between 1884

and 1894. The inscription 'Dem Deutschen Volke' (To the German People) was added in 1915. In 1918, the Weimar Republic was declared by Philipp Scheidemann from the building. The controversial fire in 1933 which destroyed the plenary hall was blamed on the Communists, and thus aided the Nazis' rise to power.

Further damaged during the Second World War and partially restored between 1957 and 1972, the building was used by the Berlin department of the Bundestag, as well as being a conference and exhibition centre. In December 1990, following reunification, the first meeting, of the newly elected parliament was held here. In 1995, Christo and his wife Jeanne-Claude wrapped the entire building in white fabric for two weeks, shortly before the work began to transform the building to the requirements of the reunited German Parliament. The commission was given to the English architect Sir Norman Foster.

The sophisticated glass dome with viewing gallery is open to the public and also provides natural light and ventilation to the parliamentary chamber below. The first meeting of the Parliament in the refurbished building was held in April 1999.

13. SHELL-HAUS
Reichpietschufer

This striking brilliant white building zigzagging along the banks of the Landwehrkanal, was designed by Emil Fahrenkamp and built during the Weimar Republic in 1930–31. Badly damaged during the war, reconstruction started in 1997 after conservationists insisted that the work should preserve faithfully the original look of the exterior and interior. The work of renovation was made difficult due to the fact that this was one of the first buildings to use a steel frame construction and wrap-around windows.

14. NEUE NATIONALGALERIE

Potsdamer Straße

At the age of seventy-five, Mies van der Rohe returned from exile to Berlin to accept the commission to design his one and only exhibition space. The massive steel roof is supported by eight slender columns on a raised stone-clad platform; the interior is on full view behind the uninterrupted glazed walls. Part of the Kulturforum, the gallery, home to the nation's collection of modern art, was built between 1965 and 1968.

15. St.-Matthäus-Kirche
Matthäikirchplatz

The church was built between 1844 and 1846 in Italian Romanesque style to the design of Friedrich August Stüler, and once stood in the middle of a small square. Threatened by demolition in 1939 to make way for Albert Speer's Germania Metropolis – the proposed new city of the Nazis, it was badly damaged during the war, but was restored and is now part of the developing Kulturforum.

16. PHILHARMONIE UND KAMMERMUSIKSAAL
Herbert-von-Karajan-Straße

Although forming a single unit, the two adjacent concert halls were designed by different architects: the Philharmonie by Hans Scharoun in 1960, and the Kammermusiksaal, based on sketches left by Scharoun, by Edgar Wisniewski in 1984. The two venues are connected by a common foyer. In both halls the orchestra's podium

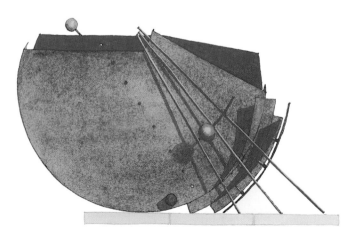

occupies centre stage, around which the seating is arranged in ascending tiers. The organic form of the building follows the functional interior, the gold-anodised façade being a recognisable Berlin landmark.

The world famous Berlin Philharmonic Orchestra founded in 1882 is based here, while the smaller hall is used for performances of chamber music.

17. BRANDENBURGER TOR
Pariser Platz

The symbol of Berlin, of peace, of victory, of division and of the reunification of the city. This, the only remaining gate to the city, was designed by Carl Gotthard Langhans. Work started in 1778 and ended in 1795, when the last of the sculpted panels was put in place. The quadriga, a two-wheeled chariot drawn by four horses and driven by the Goddess of Peace, is by Johann Gottfried Schadow, and was positioned on top of the gate in 1793. The pavilions on either side were used by guards and customs officers.

During the French occupation of Berlin in 1806, the quadriga was dismantled and taken to Paris; on its return in 1814 it was declared to represent Victory, and suitable emblems were added to the statue.

The Third Reich held their celebrations here, as did the victorious Soviet Army. In 1961 the East German government separated the two halves of the city by building a wall in the shadows of the Brandenburg Gate. It was fitting that in 1989 the first sections of the Berlin Wall were torn down at this very spot.

18. HUMBOLDT-UNIVERSITÄT
Unter den Linden

Founded in 1810 on the initiative of Wilhelm von Humboldt, a lawyer and politician, this is the oldest university in Berlin. It was named in honour of von Humboldt in 1949. The former Stadtpalais was constructed for Prince Heinrich of Prussia in 1753 to complete the northern side of the Forum Fridericianum.

The two marble statues by Paul Otto are of Wilhelm von Humboldt holding a book, and of the famous explorer Alexander von Humboldt sitting on a globe.

Hermann Helmholtz

Alexander von Humboldt

19. Neue Wache

Unter den Linden

The various names given to this small structure in the centre of Berlin is a poignant illustration of the passage of recent history. Considered to be the finest example of Neo-Classical architecture, the building, once a royal guardhouse, was designed by Karl Friedrich Schinkel and built between 1816 and 1818. In 1930 it was redesigned by Heinrich Tessenow as a memorial hall to the victims of the First World War. Under the Nazis it became a pantheon for the heroic dead.

Following the damage of the Second World War, the building was reconstructed in 1958 by the East German Government and renamed Memorial to the Victims of Fascism and Militarism. In 1993 the reunited Germany named the monument the Memorial to the Victims of War and Tyranny. Inside the building is an eternal flame, and a copy of *Pieta the Christian* by Käthe Kollwitz who lost her son in the First World War.

20. STAATSOPER
Unter den Linden

Built by Georg Wenzeslaus von Knobelsdorff between 1741 and 1743 for Friedrich the Great, this was the first building of the intended Forum Fridericianum. Destroyed by fire, it was restored by Carl Ferdinand Langhans in 1843. After extensive war damage, it was rebuilt again between 1952 and 1955.

One of the great opera houses of the world and certainly one of the most beautiful, Otto Nicolai's *The Merry Wives of Windsor*, a joyous German opera, was first performed here in 1849, conducted by the composer.

21. ALTE BIBLIOTHEK
Bebelplatz

On the west side of Bebelplatz stands one of the city's most beautiful Baroque buildings, the Royal or Old Library. It was built for Friedrich the Great around 1775 from plans by Georg Christian Unger, again as part of the planned Forum Fridericianum. The unusual concave façade of the building with Corinthian pilasters and heraldic shields is now

restored, and houses the Humboldt University Library. The square in front of the Library, once known as Opernplatz, was the site of the infamous book burning by the Nazis on 10 May 1933, when some 25,000 books written by enemies of the Third Reich were put to flames. A monument at the centre of the square commemorates the event.

22. St.-Hedwigs-Kathedrale
Bebelplatz

Built at the instigation of Friedrich the Great for the Silesian Roman Catholics in Berlin, the Cathedral was built between 1747 and 1773 to the design of Georg Wenzeslaus Knobelsdorff and loosely based on the Pantheon in Rome. Additional work continued until the late 1880s. Heavily damaged during the war, it was rebuilt between 1952 and 1963, the original dome being replaced by a reinforced concrete structure.

23. Französischer Dom

Gendarmenmarkt

Built to serve the Huguenot community expelled from France in 1685, the original church was designed by Louis Cayart and Abraham Quesnay and built between 1701 and 1705. The portico and the high tower, designed by Carl von Gontard, were added some eighty years later. Since restoration work was completed in 1984 this has been the home of the Huguenot Museum.

The 60-bell carillon in the tower rings out three times a day.

The Schiller monument

24. KONZERTHAUS
Gendarmenmarkt

The Konzerthaus, together with the Französicher and Deutscher Doms on the Gendarmenmarkt, form the most beautiful ensemble of buildings in Berlin. The Konzerthaus was designed as a theatre by Berlin's best known architect, Karl Friedrich Schinkel, and was built between 1818 to 1821 to replace the burned down National Theatre. Badly damaged during the Second World War, the

building was restored and reopened in 1984. The interior was redesigned to accommodate the building's new function as a concert hall, home of the Berlin Symphony Orchestra.

The marble monument to Friedrich Schiller in front of the theatre is by Reinhold Begas; it was erected in 1869.

25. DEUTSCHER DOM
Gendarmenmarkt

The original German Protestant Reformed church was designed by Martin Grünberg and built in 1708. The domed tower was added in 1875 by Carl von Gontard to match the one on the Französicher Dom, completing the symmetry of the Gendarmenmarkt. The Church burned down in 1945, but the exterior has been faithfully restored to its original splendour. The interior was remodelled as an exhibition space by Jürgen Pleuser, the work completed in 1996.

26. ALTES MUSEUM
Am Lustgarten

Designed by Karl Friedrich Schinkel, this most beautiful Neo-Classical museum was built between 1822 and 1830. The museum was purpose built to house the returning works of art from the royal collection, taken to Paris by Napoleon's troops. The façade is dominated by the monumental colonnade of eighteen Ionic columns. The central rotunda is based on the Pantheon in Rome. Since 1988 the museum has displayed a magnificent collection of Greek and Roman antiquities.

27. Alte Nationalgalerie
Bodestraße

The architect Friedrich August Stüler designed the building after sketches given to him by Friedrich Wilhelm IV. Built between 1866 and 1876, the gallery was originally home to the collection of Joachim Wagener, a Berlin businessman. The temple-like building on a high platform is reached by a double staircase, with an equestrian statue of Friedrich Wilhelm IV at the top. The gallery now displays 19th century art, as well as the collection of Romantic art from Charlottenburg Palace.

28. BERLINER DOM

Am Lustgarten

The first Protestant Cathedral was built on this site in 1750 as the Court church of the Hohenzollern dynasty, replacing the existing Dominican church. In 1860 the building was partially redesigned by Karl Friedrich Schinkel. The present Neo-Baroque structure, dating fronm 1905, is the work of Julius Raschdorff. The Cathedral was renovated after extensive damage suffered during the war, and was inaugurated in 1996.

29. SONY-CENTER
Potsdamer Platz

Once the busiest city square, the area lay flattened by war and undisturbed under the Berlin Wall for some fifty years. With the reunification of the city, Potsdamer Platz presented a unique challenge to architects and planners to develop such a large and important site. The competition in 1991 was won by the office of Hilmer & Sattler, with their European-style, medium-high development of dense streets, alleys and squares. The only exception allowed is at the centre of the site next to the Potsdamer Platz S-Bahn station. The Sony Center itself, built on a triangular site, is by the architect Helmut Jahn. The buildings are arranged around the oval-shaped Sony Plaza entertainment centre, with its tent-like roof, supported by steel rods and cables, the focal point.

Debis Haus

30. Jüdisches Museum
Lindenstraße

One of the most spectacular post-war buildings, the museum was designed by Daniel Libeskind and built between 1993 and 1999. The broken plan of irregular shapes zigzagging around the site represent the history of Jews in Berlin in a most profound and thoughtful manner. The building is approached through an underground passage from the adjacent Berlin Museum, a Baroque-style building designed by Philipp Gerlach in 1735 as administrative offices.

The Berlin Museum

31. ALDO-ROSSI-BLOCK
Quartier Schützenstraße

The little that remained of the original block after the war was sterilised for years by the Berlin Wall. Preserving the single remaining building, Italian architect Aldo Rossi designed an entire block of individual buildings, taking as his inspiration the historical examples

of urban structures: the roofscape is Parisian, while some of the façades are influenced by the Palazzo Farnese in Rome. The block provides a mixture of residential and commercial uses, its brightly painted structure livening up this area near Checkpoint Charlie.

Der Roland

32. MÄRKISCHES MUSEUM
Am Köllnischen Park

Designed by Berlin's city architect Ludwig Hoffmann, and built between 1899 and 1908, this complex set of buildings is intended to illustrate the various styles of Mark Brandenburg, and to display the history of Berlin and the Brandenburg region. In the surrounding park is a bear pit with a resident live bear, the official mascot of Berlin.

33. NIKOLAIKIRCHE
Nikolaikirchplatz

Dominating the surrounding Nikolai district of restored old houses, are the twin towers of the oldest sacred building in Berlin. Built at the beginning of the thirteenth century, restored in the 1870s and rebuilt after war damage in time for Berlin's 750th anniversary in 1987, the building now houses a museum of the history of the city.

Neptunbrunnen

34. BERLINER RATHAUS
Rathausstraße

Inspired by Italian Renaissance architecture, the building was designed by Hermann Friedrich Waesemann. It was built between 1861 and 1869 and is known as the Rotes Rathaus for the red bricks used on the façade. Restored after war damage, the building first housed the East Berlin authorities, and since reunification the office of the mayor of Berlin. The *Neptunbrunnen*, moved to the square in front of the Rathaus in 1969, was created by Reinhold Begas in 1886.

35. FERNSEHTURM

Alexanderplatz

The second tallest structure in Europe, with a viewing platform and revolving restaurant in the metal sphere at the top, the TV tower was designed by a team of German architects and built in 1969. Suitably positioned facing the tower, symbol of socialist achievement, are the combined statues of Marx and Engels by Ludwig Engelhardt.

Marx & Engels

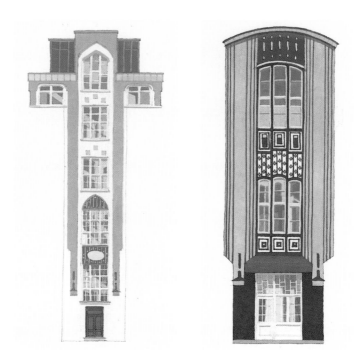

36. HACKESCHE HÖFE
Rosenthaler Straße

This fascinating series of eight interlinking courtyards, designed by Kurt Berndt and August Endell around 1906, is an exciting example of Jugendstil architecture. Through the recently restored façade the courtyards follow on with restaurants, shops, galleries, a cinema, the Hackesche Hoftheater, and apartments and offices on the upper floors. The first courtyard is decorated with a geometric design in glazed tiles to the design of August Endell.

37. NEUE SYNAGOGE
Oranienburger Straße

The biggest and most splendid synagogue in Germany was designed by Eduard Knoblauch and Friedrich August Stüler and opened in 1866. It is built in a Moorish style, but with innovative use of iron in the roof structure and galleries. The synagogue was set on fire during Kristallnacht in November 1938, further damaged by the war, and was demolished in 1958. Reconstruction started in 1988 and the completed building with its restored gilded dome opened as the Centrum Judaicum in 1995.

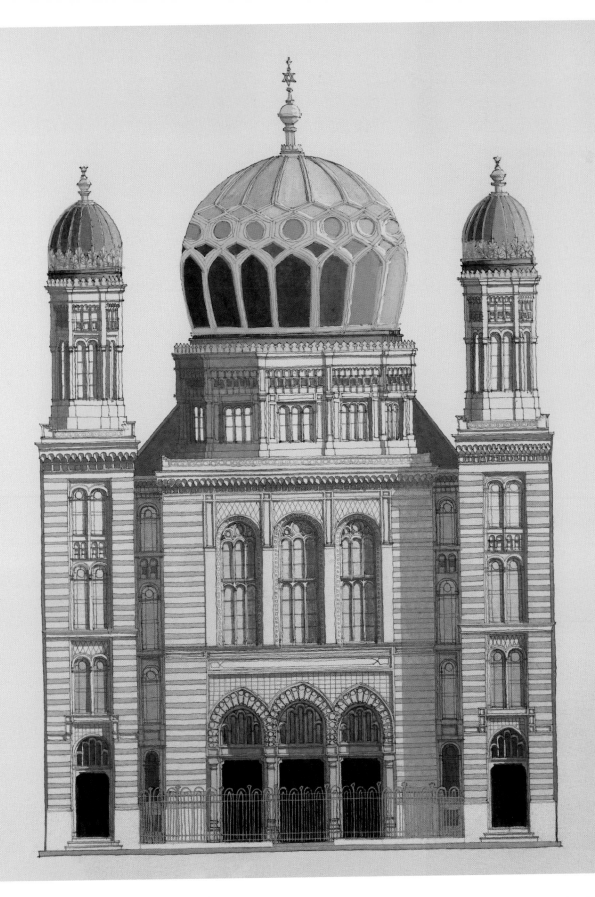

38. FRIEDRICHSTADTPALAST
Friedrichstraße

The present building replaced a much loved theatre for 5,000 people. The original building suffered bomb damage, was condemned and replaced by the new building in the early 1980s. The huge interior is used in turn as a theatre, circus, ice rink, swimming pool. The stage is equipped with every technical aid. A small cabaret theatre for 240 people is also part of the complex.

39. DEUTSCHES THEATER
Schumannstraße

Constructed in 1849/50, the building was designed by Eduard Titz to house the Friedrich-Wilhelm Städtisches Theater. In 1883, after major reconstruction it was renamed the Deutsches Theater, and became famous under its new director Otto Brahm. Max Reinhardt started his career here as an actor, becoming director in 1905. Bertolt Brecht wrote plays for the Deutsches Theater and became its director with the Berliner Ensemble after the War.

40. HAMBURGER BAHNHOF
Invalidenstraße

One of the oldest railway termini, it was built in 1847 but soon became too small to serve its purpose and was closed in 1884. First opened as a transport museum in 1906, the wing to the courtyard was added between 1911 and 1916.

Since 1966 the building has been the home of the Museum of Contemporary Art. The vaulted central hall is a perfect environment for the display of large canvases and installations.

BIBLIOGRAPHY

Berlin: A guide to recent architecture, Ellipsis London Ltd., 1997

Berlin, Dorling Kindersley Travel Guide, 2000

Berlin in your pocket, Michelin, 1998

Berlin, Lonely Planet, 2000

Ulrich Eckhardt, *Berlin, Open City*, Nicolai, 1999

Thomas W. Gaehtgens, *Charlottenburg Palace, Berlin*, Fondation Paribas, 1995

Andrew Gumbel, *Berlin*, Cadogan City Guides, 1991

H. Karasek and T. Friedrich, photography M. Haddenhorst, *Berlin, Bilder einer Stadt*, Nicolai, 1998

Bernhard Schneider, *Daniel Libeskind Jüdisches Museum Berlin*, Prestel Verlag, 1999

Debis Haus, Potsdamer Platz

Andras Kaldor Gallery
15 Newcomen Road
Dartmouth, Devon TQ6 9BN, UK
Telephone 01803 833874
Fax 01803 835161
e-mail andras@kaldor.com
website www.kaldor.com

Andras Kaldor, seen here in his gallery in Dartmouth, England, surrounded by some of his architectural paintings. In his art he successfully combines the disciplines of painting and architecture. He has portrayed famous buildings and monuments from Berlin to San Francisco and his works have been exhibited on both sides of the Atlantic.

In the same series by Andras Kaldor, and also published by the Antique Collectors' Club, are *Great Opera Houses – Masterpieces of Architecture*, and *New York – Masterpieces of Architecture*.